Roar!

World of Wonder
PREHISTORIC
ANIMALS

SALARIYA

Published in Great Britain in MMX by
Book House, an imprint of
The Salariya Book Company Ltd
25 Marlborough Place,
Brighton BN1 1UB

HB ISBN: 978-1-907184-12-3
PB ISBN: 978-1-907184-13-0

A CIP catalogue record for this book is available
from the British Library.

Printed and bound in China.
Printed on paper from sustainable sources.

Editor: Elizabeth Branch

Author: Carolyn Franklin has a special interest in
natural history and has written many books on the
subject, including *Life in the Wetlands* in the
WHAT ON EARTH? series, *Lion Journal* and *Gorilla
Journal* in the ANIMAL JOURNAL series.

Artist: John Francis's work ranges widely over all areas
of wildlife portrayal from the demands of scientific
exactness to the more loosely drawn children's books for
which he is also known.

Scientific Consultant: John Cooper is a geologist, and
for many years was Keeper of the Booth Museum of
Natural History. He has written children's books on
dinosaurs, volcanoes and earthquakes as well as acting
as consultant for many more.

Educational Consultant: Monica Hughes is an
experienced educational advisor and author of more than
one hundred books for young children. She has been
headteacher of a primary school, primary advisory
teacher, and senior lecturer in early childhood education.

Visit our website at **www.book-house.co.uk**
or go to **www.salariya.com**
for **free** electronic versions of:
You Wouldn't Want to be an Egyptian Mummy!
You Wouldn't Want to be a Roman Gladiator!
Avoid Joining Shackleton's Polar Expedition!
Avoid Sailing on a 19th-Century Whaling Ship!

World of Wonder
Prehistoric Animals

Written by
Carolyn Franklin

Illustrated by
John Francis

BOOK HOUSE

Contents

What were prehistoric animals?

About 65 million years ago, dinosaurs became **extinct**. About three-quarters of all plants and animals also died out. Many scientists believe that this extinction was caused when a comet hit the Earth. This book is about the prehistoric animals that lived in the millions of years that came after this extinction.

Desmostylus
(Dez-mo-STY-lus)

Why are they called prehistoric animals?

They are called prehistoric animals because they lived long ago, before people had begun to write about nature and animals.

What did prehistoric animals eat?

Prehistoric animals were either plant-eaters or meat-eaters. Animals that eat mostly meat are called **carnivores**. The largest meat-eating carnivore ever was Andrewsarchus!

Andrewsarchus
(And-rooz-ARK-us)

Grrr!

Andrewsarchus may have hunted and killed other animals. It may also have eaten the bodies of dead animals.

Andrewsarchus grew to be about 3.4 metres long and was up to 1.5 metres tall. Its huge head was nearly 1 metre long.

How did Andrewsarchus use its teeth?

Andrewsarchus used its sharp front teeth for tearing at flesh. Its flatter back teeth were used to crush and crunch bones.

Scale

The scale shows the size of each animal beside a man.

Indricotherium
(In-drik-oh-THEER-ee-um)

Munch

Which was the largest prehistoric mammal?

Indricotherium was the largest land **mammal**! It weighed more than 4 elephants, was about 8 metres long and 5.5 metres tall. Indricotherium was a **herbivore**, an animal that mainly eats plants.

The body of an Indricotherium was similar to a present-day rhinoceros, but it had a longer neck, long legs and no horn.

Scale

Indricotherium lived in parts of Asia, from 30 million to 20 million years ago.

True or False?
Indricotherium had five toes on each foot.

Answers on page 31

9

Did any prehistoric animals have big tusks?

Woolly mammoths had two **tusks** which were up to 5 metres long. They may have used their tusks to clear away snow, so they could eat the plants beneath.

Woolly mammoths lived 50,000 years ago during an **ice age**. It was very cold. Huge masses of ice called **glaciers** covered large parts of Europe and North America. The woolly mammoth's fur coat helped to keep it warm and dry.

10

A woolly mammoth was about the same size as an African elephant. Under its fur, a thick layer of fat kept the mammoth safe from the cold.

Woolly mammoth

Scale

A woolly mammoth was very hairy. It had two layers of fur. The top layer was long, shaggy hair and underneath it the fur was thick and woolly.

True or False?

Woolly mammoths ate 225 kilograms of plants a day!

Answers on page 31

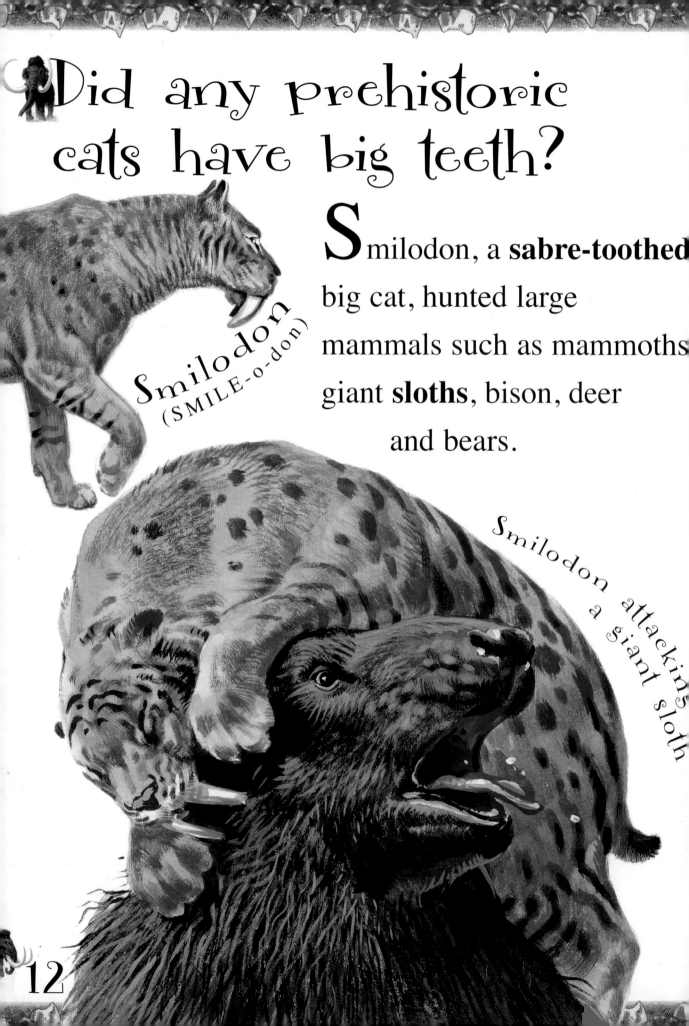

Did any prehistoric cats have big teeth?

Smilodon, a **sabre-toothed** big cat, hunted large mammals such as mammoths, giant **sloths**, bison, deer and bears.

Smilodon (SMILE-o-don)

Smilodon attacking a giant sloth

Answers on page 31

True or False?
The name 'Smilodon'
means 'big smile'.

Smilodon lived in North and
South America. A Smilodon
may have been over 2 metres
long and 1.2 metres tall. It
may have weighed as much
as 400 kilograms.

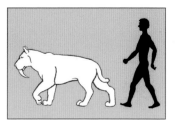

Scale

Smilodon's sabre
teeth grew up to
28 centimetres long.
Its jaws could open
very wide so
Smilodon could use
these teeth to stab
or kill its **prey**.

Smilodon's
skeleton

Did any prehistoric animals have antlers?

Megaloceros were giant deer. The male Megaloceros had huge **antlers**. These could be up to 3.7 metres from tip to tip. The Megaloceros used their antlers to fight each other, just like male red deer do today.

Megaloceros lived in woodland areas, but only where the trees were far enough apart for their antlers to pass through. They ate grass and other plants.

Scale

The name 'Megaloceros' means 'great horn'. Megaloceros is also known as the Irish elk.

Megaloceros
(Meg-a-LOSS-er-oss)

These giant deer lived in Europe between 400,000 and 9,500 years ago.

Were there prehistoric birds?

Gastornis and Phorusrhacos were prehistoric birds. They were scary and are known as 'terror birds'. Both birds were huge, and neither could fly. They were meat-eaters that hunted small mammals.

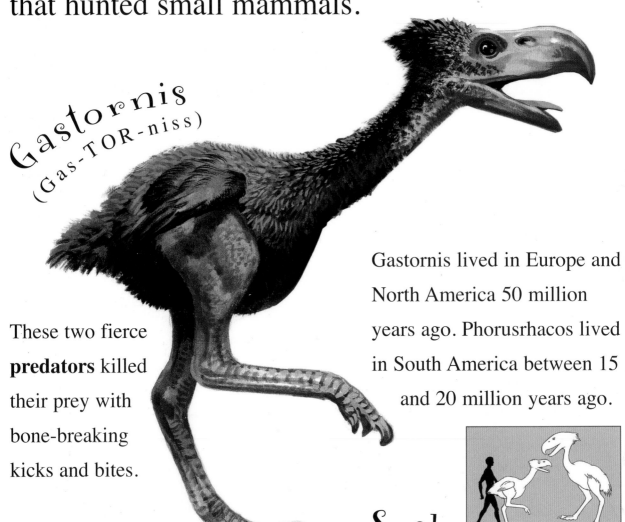

Gastornis
(Gas-TOR-niss)

These two fierce **predators** killed their prey with bone-breaking kicks and bites.

Gastornis lived in Europe and North America 50 million years ago. Phorusrhacos lived in South America between 15 and 20 million years ago.

Scale

Phorusrhacos was the biggest of the 'terror birds'. It was 3 metres tall, with long legs and a massive hooked beak.

Pachyrukhos
(Pa-kee-RU-koss)

Phorusrhacos
(For-us-RACK-oss)

Phorusrhacos was probably the fastest animal of its time!

True or False?

Some birds ate horses.

Answers on page 31

How did prehistoric animals change?

Megatherium was a big sloth that **evolved** over time. Food was plentiful. When bigger, stronger sloths mated, they created stronger young. After many thousands of years the Megatherium grew larger and stronger.

Megatherium
(Meg-a-THEER-ee-um)

Scale

Did Megatherium eat meat?

No, Megatherium was a herbivore. But it may have eaten dead animals that it found, or killed prey itself with its huge claws and strong arms.

True or False?

Megatherium could
run very fast.

Answers on page 31

Megatherium had long
dark hair and could
walk on two legs like
a bear. It grew up to
6 metres long and
weighed 3.8 tonnes.

Megatherium lived
in South America
between 1.9 million
and 8,000 years ago.

Scale

Did prehistoric animals live in the sea?

Yes, Ambulocetus did – it was one of the first sea mammals. Its name means 'walking whale'. It could walk on land and swim in the sea.

Ambulocetus
(Am-byu-lo-SEE-tus)

Ambulocetus lay in wait for passing mammals. Once it caught its prey it would drag it into the water to drown it.

True or False?
Ambulocetus used its jaws to hear! ?
? ?

Answers on page 31

Grrr!

How did it swim?

Ambulocetus had long webbed toes and strong back legs for swimming. Its eyes and nostrils were on top of its head. It could see and breathe while partly underwater.

21

Megalodon
(MEG-a-lo-don)

What was the biggest prehistoric shark?

A Megalodon! It was twice as long as a modern great white shark. Megalodon had a huge mouth that was 2 metres wide. It used its strong jaws to grip its prey.

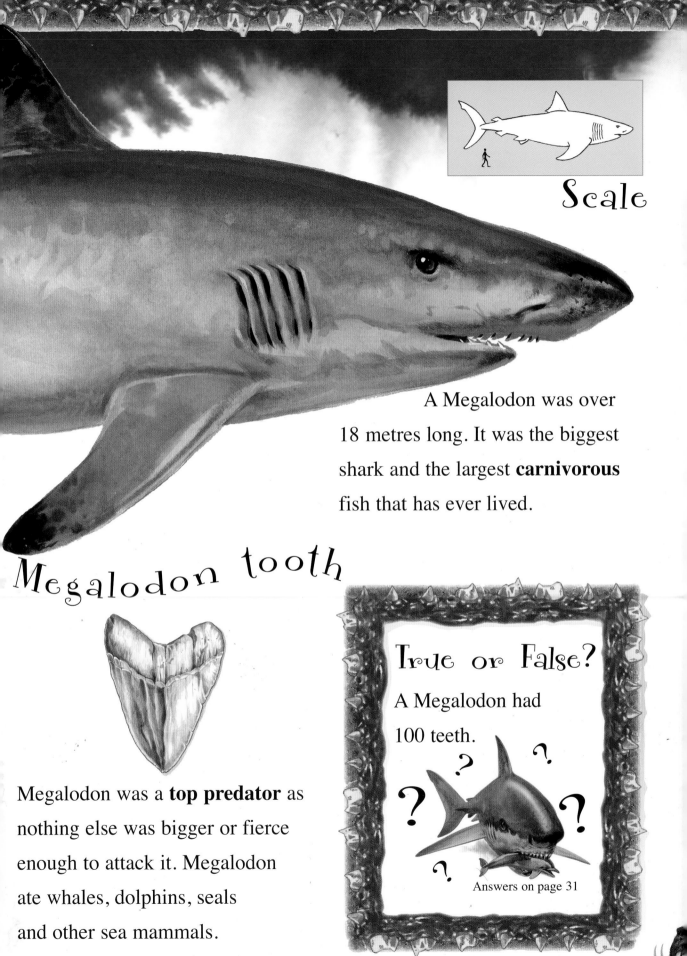

A Megalodon was over 18 metres long. It was the biggest shark and the largest **carnivorous** fish that has ever lived.

Megalodon tooth

Megalodon was a **top predator** as nothing else was bigger or fierce enough to attack it. Megalodon ate whales, dolphins, seals and other sea mammals.

True or False?

A Megalodon had 100 teeth.

Answers on page 31

23

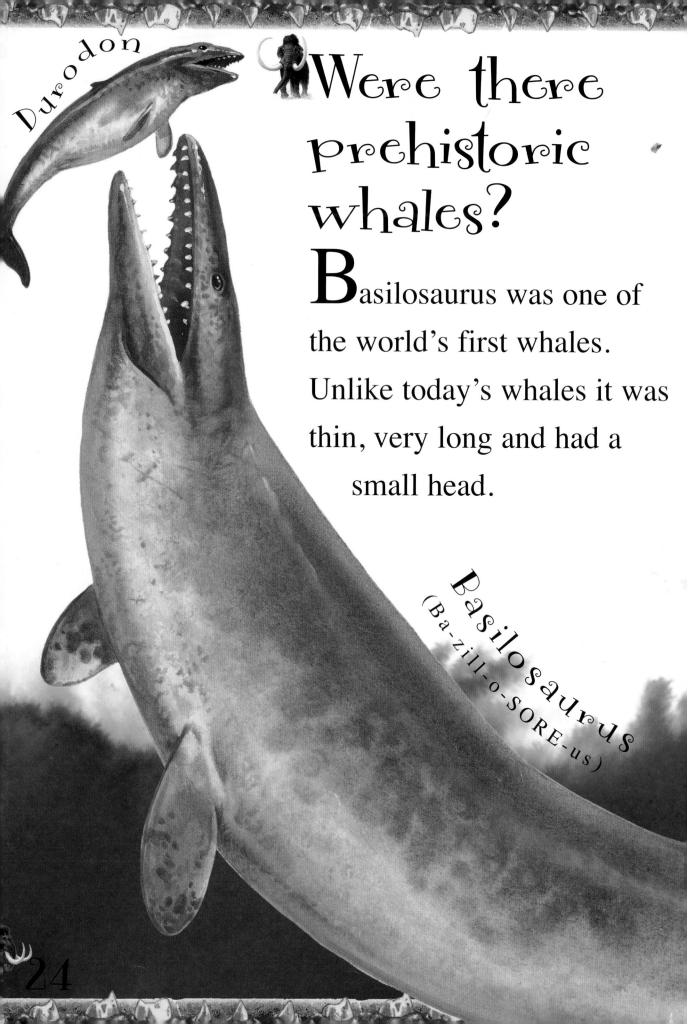

Durodon

Were there prehistoric whales?

Basilosaurus was one of the world's first whales. Unlike today's whales it was thin, very long and had a small head.

Basilosaurus
(Ba-zill-o-SORE-us)

Basilosaurus lived in the warm seas around Africa, Europe and North America from 45 to 36 million years ago.

How did it swim?

Basilosaurus moved its tail up and down to swim. It could hear and see well underwater, so it could easily catch and eat fish, squid, turtles, sharks and other, smaller whales.

Basilosaurus grew up to 21 metres long. Its powerful jaws were packed with teeth for biting and slicing!

Scale

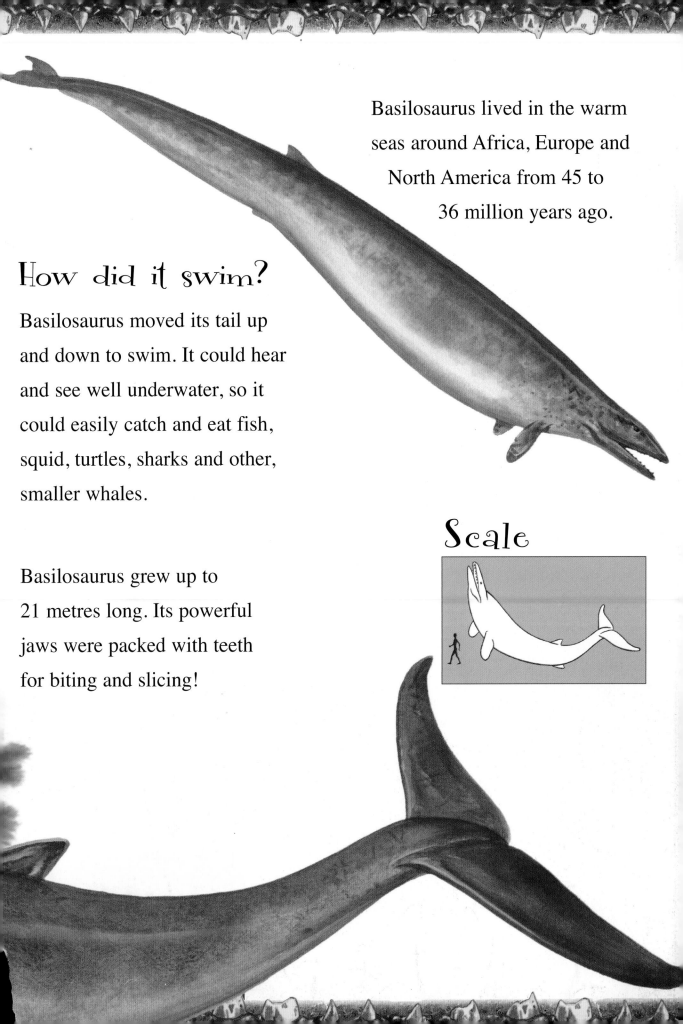

What happened to the prehistoric animals?

Although prehistoric animals became extinct, many evolved into present-day animals such as elephants, whales and tigers. During the ice ages, cold temperatures killed most of the plants. So the herbivores died from **starvation**. Meat-eating carnivores feasted on their remains until they too ran out of food.

Other animals couldn't survive when their **environment** changed. Mammoths moved south, away from the cold grasslands they fed on. The mammoths met early human hunters who began to hunt and kill them for food.

Hunters dug traps which the mammoths fell into, then killed them with spears.

Coelodonta was a woolly rhino. It also died out when the grasslands it lived on disappeared in the last ice age.

Early humans hunted Coelodonta. They used sharp stone tools to cut the woolly rhino's body into pieces.

Coelodonta
(See-loh-DON-ta)

True or False?
A woolly rhino's horns were made of bone.

Answers on page 31

Scale

How do we know about prehistoric animals?

Scientists study the bones of prehistoric animals that they find buried in the ground. Sometimes a complete skeleton is found. Scientists compare these skeletons with the bones of present-day animals. This helps them to discover the size and speed of prehistoric animals, how they lived and what they ate.

Indricotherium skeleton

Are there pictures?

In France, caves have been found with paintings of woolly rhinos on their walls. Early humans painted them 30,000 years ago.

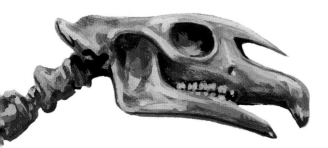

What is a fossil?

A fossil is the remains of an animal or plant that died long ago. Over thousands or many millions of years the remains turn into stone.

Sometimes the whole body of a prehistoric animal has been found. This baby mammoth was found **preserved** in the icy ground of Siberia, northern Russia.

Baby mammoth

Glossary

Antlers The pair of bony growths that develop each year on the head of male deer.

Carnivore An animal that eats mostly meat.

Carnivorous Mainly eating meat.

Environment The area in which something lives.

Evolved Slowly changed over millions of years.

Extinct No longer alive anywhere in the world.

Glacier A huge mass of ice that slowly moves over the land.

Habitat The place where something normally lives or occurs.

Herbivore An animal that mainly eats plants.

Ice age Any one of the very cold periods during which glaciers covered much of the Earth.

Mammal An animal that is born alive, then fed by its mother's milk.

Predator An animal that kills then eats its prey.

Preserved Kept without being changed.

Prey Animals that are killed and eaten by other animals.

Sabre-toothed Having teeth that look like sabres or small swords.

Sloth A slow-moving mammal that only eats plants.

Starvation Extreme hunger over a long time.

Top predator An animal that is not usually caught and eaten by any other animal that lives in its habitat.

Tusk A very long front tooth of certain mammals. The tusk sticks out even when the mouth is closed.

Answers

Page 9 **FALSE!** Indricotherium had three toes on each foot. The toes were hoofed like a present-day rhino.

Page 11 **TRUE!** A woolly mammoth ate about 225 kilograms of plants, grass, shrubs and trees each day.

Page 13 **FALSE!** The name 'Smilodon' means 'knife tooth'. Smilodon's fangs were long and thin, rather than round like the teeth of present-day tigers.

Page 17 **TRUE!** Gastornis could have eaten a horse. When Gastornis lived, horses were much smaller than they are now; about the size of a large domestic cat.

Page 19 **FALSE!** Megatherium was very slow-moving, rather like present-day sloths.

Page 21 **TRUE!** Ambulocetus did use its jaws to hear! It didn't have ears on the outside of its head. Ambulocetus used its jawbone to pick up vibrations, just as modern whales do.

Page 23 **FALSE!** Megalodon may have had hundreds of teeth. Most sharks have between 3 and 5 rows of teeth at a time. As teeth are lost, broken or worn away the other rows of teeth grow round to replace them.

Page 27 **FALSE!** The woolly rhino's horns were made of hair. The hairs were stuck together, making the horns solid.

Megalodon

Index

(Illustrations are shown in **bold** type).